Success with Sanity

Planning for Effective Curriculum Implementation

Mary E Condon, NBCT

ISBN-10: 0615543618
ISBN-13: 978-0615543611

Success with Sanity

Planning for Effective Curriculum Implementation

Mary E Condon, NBCT

For Mother, who was always
the wind beneath my wings

CONTENTS

ACKNOWLEDGMENTS

In the beginning I was, unbeknownst to me at the time, exceptionally blessed to have learned from (as a student teacher) and taught with (as a colleague) my friend Barb. Everything I know about high school planning and teaching is the result of her guidance and instruction. I am thankful for inheriting her files all those years ago and for her modeling a method of planning for engaging students in real-life experiences in the classroom. From her, I learned that teaching is not about the textbook. Without her, I'd need to read this book, not write it.

My biggest blessing during my career and the writing of this book has been my good friend Sara, whom I supervised (as a student teacher), taught with (as a colleague) and grew as a teacher and a person with the love and support of her and her family. She, along with Patrick, Luca, Joze and Mari, have saved my life at least three times (two literally, one figuratively) and, without her support and encouragement, this book would likely never have been written.

Gretchen has always been the go-to language person for any of about 10 different languages. I appreciate her willingness to provide brutally honest comments and proofreading. She has a knack of knowing the point I am trying to make, even when I can't seem to express it so others can understand. I respect, also, the proofing of my writing while allowing the words and expressions I use to stay true to the way I actually talk. She understood that I want an informal, conversational style and kept me true to it.

Finally, I need to thank my department – then and now – for providing support, encouragement and examples throughout my teaching career and the writing of this book. They have had to listen to me say almost everything I write here hundreds of times during the course of our days together. I appreciate their putting up with me and keeping me grounded.

Chapter 1
Success with Sanity?

August. So. Here we go again. The beginning-of-school workshops.   A day that I have dreaded every fall for the last 34 years. The day when our language departments from across the fifth-largest school district in the state meet together for our annual "professional development." I dread it because every year it is the same discussion.   I can write the (almost word-for-word) script for this day each year:

—   *How far did you get last year?*
—   *Chapter 3*
—   *Chapter 4.1*
—   *Chapter 4.2*
—   *We did some parts of 4.2*
—   *Chapter 4.3*

... and so on, until everyone has, with additional comments, explanations, rationale and excuses, given an answer. The conversation continues with the *hows* *a*nd the *why*s of each teacher's rationale (again, I could write the script!).   The veteran teachers have a free-for-all discussion, the point of which is to insist that each really does the right thing and we should all do it that way, too. Newer teachers wonder why they didn't know what they really *should* have taught last year, where they really were *supposed* to be at the end of the year, or why some things should have/could have been excluded. After all, they had been given a curriculum they were supposed to teach – and that is what they tried to do.   First-year teachers watch the spectacle with deer-in-the-headlights eyes, wondering what is really going on.   No truly shared decision has ever resulted from that discussion. Everyone packs his or her own ideas back into his/her head, each thinking that s/he is right, leaves, teaches as s/he always has, returns next year, and repeats. So why must this cycle continue *every* year for 34 years and counting?

Teachers, usually in isolation, begin with day one in the plan book and work forward. This method guarantees that, no matter what the decision of "*where should we end?*" is, each teacher will arrive at a different place at a different time. That kind of planning hurts students in at least five ways:

1) they may not be given the appropriate essential content required in the curriculum;
2) they have to go through the same material twice when classes change at semester time and their teacher has been "behind" the others;
3) they miss a chunk of the progression of material for the same reason;
4) teachers rush through material faster than students can properly learn;
5) and the classroom becomes a trampoline, jumping around with this here and that there.

And perhaps, as it does for me, the beginning of the year brings two new classes to teach ('preps') that need to be written and implemented within the next two weeks. YIKES! I am ending my teaching career much as I began, with five different preps to teach; this time one is new (but a blend of two others), one is an entirely new curriculum, one is my second time through a course that was brand new for me last year, and two are courses that I have been teaching forever. Effective planning is essential if I am to be successful in the classroom while maintaining my sanity!

As my purpose for this book is to concentrate on planning, I'll start with the assumption that a written curriculum is in already in place for teachers when they arrive in the classroom for the first time. I'll also assume that core objectives are identified and appropriate assessments are written. It is even possible that specific learning opportunities/activities are laid out in the curriculum, although this would likely be rare. In other words, I'm assuming that all of the basic ingredients are there, just as they would be listed in a recipe.

Let's say I provide you with this list: flour, sugar, eggs, baking soda, milk or water and butter; nuts if desired. Now bake. Do you even know what the final result is supposed to be? Even if I were to also provide the quantities of ingredients my guess is that you would end up with a different, possibly inedible result than what I had hoped for and/or expected when I gave you that list.

So it is in the classroom. I'm assuming that all of the ingredients necessary to teach what is supposed to be taught are provided when the teacher walks in the room. It is not, however, uncommon to walk into a classroom and discover that you're missing an egg or a cup of flour – or the whole recipe! When baking, we can run to our neighbors to see if they can give/lend us a missing ingredient. We can run to our neighbors in the school for some assistance, as well. We would not demand (hopefully!) that the neighbor would take over all the baking for us if we ask for them to lend us an ingredient. Nor would we, most likely, want to give our neighbors that power – after all, if the product were to turn out well, we would want to get the credit we deserve! Keep this in mind the next time you go to a colleague for the equivalent of a cup of flour or an egg – do not count on the colleague having the time or inclination to take over the planning for you. There is a difference in ingredients, as well. When you borrow a cup of flour or an egg, you know exactly what you are getting and how to use it in a recipe. Help in the form of an idea, a plan or an activity from you colleague will usually be specific to him or her and may well be something you don't know how to use. Ask for some assistance when necessary, but don't rely on that assistance to get the job done the way you want it to be done.

Okay, we now have all the ingredients on the list, so what is still missing from the recipe? The directions! The manner in which the recipe should be implemented. I remember a time as a young girl helping my mother to bake Christmas cookies, specifically spritz and sugar cut-outs. I could not understand why there were instructions for the order of things to mix the dough. I thought that if all the ingredients were present, we should just be able to throw them all in a bowl, mix and bake. Have you ever tried that? Imagine: a cold, solid stick of butter, 3 cups of flour, some sugar and a whole egg dumped together in a bowl. Now, turn that into cookie dough! I learned – and fast -- why one creams the sugar and fat plus egg, sifts all the flour together with other dry ingredients and then works in the flour (and nuts, if desired). I eventually became a fairly good baker. Had I not been shown a better method than dump and pour, I would not yet be baking edible cookies.

Throughout our education classes in college, we all learned and practiced writing, implementing and reviewing lesson plans (our recipes for the classroom). So why, then, is it that teachers find it difficult to *implement* curriculum in a sane, realistic, articulated manner?

I believe the answer to that question is that teachers are simply unaware of effective strategies (think creaming the sugar and butter) for the implementation of the curriculum they are given (or have written). Teachers tend to be more comfortable planning one lesson at a time, or one week at a time, or even one unit at a time going forward. They do this without a year-long, semester-long or trimester-long focus and, often, without knowing effective strategies for the *implementation* of the whole curriculum. Without those strategies, successful planning for curriculum implementation may be doomed, no matter how well written the curriculum may be.

As teachers, we all learned and practiced in college various techniques not only for lesson planning, but also for curriculum design and assessment of learning. Emphasis is traditionally placed on the *development* of the curriculum, not its implementation. We know *what* we are supposed to "cover" throughout the year or the semester. However, real teachers in real classrooms are rarely given guidance in how to go about the practical *implementation* of the curriculum. For one reason or another they are left to their own devices. Principals presume that teachers should know how to plan for implementation (they were in the same boat many years ago when they were teaching and probably don't remember what it felt like to be dropped into the middle of the territory with a map but no plan). The veteran teachers who could help are busy trying to keep their own sanity and, perhaps, not very good at planning and implementation, either. Teachers are sometimes reluctant to ask for help from colleagues, as they think it would be a sign of incompetence. And some veteran teachers even think that the new person should sink or swim alone – after all, that's how they had to learn.

As in baking cookies, even the very best list of ingredients in the curriculum will suffer without a good strategy for its implementation. Even the best curriculum will remain a document that teachers refer to (if they can even find it) but not really use .

To find something that matches actual classroom practice we usually need to look at the current textbook. And when we do, we'll often find stressed and anxious teachers trying to fit all the curriculum, ... er......, I mean, textbook, into a given time frame. The end result? Curriculum = textbook; textbook = curriculum. Textbook pages 1 to 252 = those 252 pages of content. This is not what Curriculum 101 in education training usually presents as the way to go. But strategies for implementing the information necessary from those 252 pages are usually overlooked.

My subject expertise is acquiring Spanish as a second language. If I were to look at (and believe) the above equations, it would seem to me that the "curriculum" for the course would change every time a new textbook is adopted. *Really?* What we want students to learn about verb conjugation, vocabulary for the family, how to order in a restaurant suddenly changes when the textbook changes? *Really??* The curriculum should be the solid base of knowledge intended to be presented to students (and hopefully learned!) during their time in the classroom with the teacher. Students will not stop conjugating verbs, finding right angles or analyzing a poem simply because the textbook that presents that content does so in a different order or different manner. The curriculum is (or should be) more than a textbook package of lesson planning, curriculum design or assessment. programs. Rather, it should be the guide that the real-life teacher in the real-life classroom uses to effectively plan and implement activities and lessons so students acquire the essential knowledge and skills required in the curriculum.

In the following pages, I present seven essential strategic steps to assist real teachers in implementing their curriculum through effective planning – semester by semester, month by month, week by week and day to day. It has been my experience that these strategies will not only lead to better and more successful instruction and learning, but that the teacher can implement them while remaining sane in the classroom! Given the right tools, a teacher *can* experience success with sanity!

Throughout my teaching career, I have had the opportunity to guide several student teachers, as well as to mentor several teachers either new to teaching or new to our building or district. Most of those student teachers or new teachers have been well prepared with theory and can complete a single lesson plan without a problem. But when I ask them to show me where they are going with their lessons – why they will follow today with tomorrow, how they will articulate with the others in the department, or how they will fit everything into the trimester, most would find it impossible to explain. The necessity of planning lessons for one week at a time is overwhelming enough; they are happy to have plans in the book even a day or two in advance, particularly if there are more than two preps to plan. Consequently, instruction and learning are at the mercy of those plans – as is the sanity of the teacher.

One of my all-time favorite student teachers, Rachel, Is a particularly good example to illustrate this. She was a great teacher. She had great rapport with the students. She wrote and delivered magnificent lesson plans. Students liked her and really learned from her. But during the entire four months that she worked with me in my classroom, she just could not learn the reality of planning more than a couple of days ahead (if even that). I tried to model and teach how to sketch out a plan in advance for one week so I could see her bigger-picture plan. She relied on me for direction, (even when I wouldn't give it!), rather than to do her own planning ahead to implement the curriculum which I provided for her. For the last month of Rachel's time with me, I was insistent that she give me one week's worth of plans at a time for the classes she was teaching. Through her very last day, she just could not do it.

Other than planning for effective implementation of the curriculum, Rachel was a fabulous teacher. She was an excellent example of a well-trained and well-educated Spanish teacher who had never been exposed to the idea of planning ahead through the strategy of backward planning, until she worked with me. I know many teachers out there are just like her!   Upon completion of her student teaching, she was hired in my building as a Spanish/French teacher the following fall. Once she was personally responsible for moving her students forward from day one to day 173, she came to the realization that it *is* necessary to have that big picture to know where one is going (or better said, how to get to where one knows one *should* be going). She finally realized that without the big picture, she would drive herself crazy. She would not know what she would teach tomorrow, and would not always be prepared to teach. And would not always have ready the things that she needed to teach.   And would not have a logical flow to her lessons. And would not be on track to be where she should or would want to be at the end of the trimester.   And would not….

Throughout my many years of experience, I have found that most teachers aren't prepared to implement curriculum in a manner that can keep them on track and ensure vertical and horizontal articulation. (I use articulation here to mean curriculum mapping or spiraling instruction so that students may transfer from one teacher to another at the end of a semester or progress from year to year with no gaps in content.) It is with that in mind that I offer the following seven-step process that I have crafted over the years and have followed to successfully implement curriculum in my teaching in an attempt to maintain my sanity with multiple preps and multiple teachers responsible for the same courses. I have found that these strategies have allowed me to be a better, more organized teacher, thereby delivering better lessons and improving my impact on student learning through better planning.

Over the years, I have shared these strategies with my colleagues. Most of them have latched on to at least some of them so I know these strategies can work for others, as well as for me. We even joke among ourselves that "planning ahead" is 'illegal' in our building. Most of us are uncomfortable with the by-the seat-of-the-pants planning that has often been modeled by our administration. Several of these teachers have credited me with helping them to become better (not to mention more sane) teachers. Many of those teachers had not had the remarkable opportunity that I did when student teaching: to learn a functional framework that leads to long-term successful planning. Many teachers out there are just following a textbook, so that is what they pass on to the student teachers they supervise. Many of those who are teaching others to teach do not have the skills to teach them to plan in a comprehensive way, so the cycle of frustration continues.

I have often heard my colleagues tell the student teachers with whom I work that they are incredibly lucky to experience my strategies from the ground up. Most of those experienced teachers have spent years of their career struggling with planning. Maybe, if they were lucky, they stumbled upon a person or workshop that could show them a better way to plan so they could experience success while maintaining their sanity and providing better instruction for their students. Upon learning and trying my strategies, they now view those strategies as the way things should be done. I was, many years ago, told by a principal that I had been controlling and manipulating the members of my department. I am not afraid to share with others -- I don't think keeping secrets from your colleagues creates a healthy work environment. When I told my department what the principal had said to me, they immediately defended my actions as those of a leader with knowledge and experience to share, rather than a monster dictating what to do. The phrase Mary "controls and manipulates" comes up a lot now, as another inside joke in my department. My colleagues have told me, from the first time I shared this comment with them, that they see this as a negative statement about *them* rather than me; their inference is that they can only follow and not have ideas of their own. They are not little lambs that are sure to go wherever Mary may go. But my longevity, experience and proven success always gives us a solid place to begin.

When I was a student teacher, I didn't have any idea that I was getting unusually brilliant instruction from a very unique cooperating teacher. I presumed at that time that everyone learned as a student teacher what I did: to plan ahead and work backwards to do so. My student teaching experience involved five levels of Spanish with a textbook provided for only the first year.

My cooperating teacher, Barb, had created a curriculum for years one through five that produced incredibly above-average Spanish speakers (I was to learn with more experience). I took everything I learned then for granted. It has now become very obvious to me, however, when I see how other teachers have been taught to plan and teach, that I was extremely lucky! I want to pass along to others those strategies that have helped me to plan and implement whatever curriculum I am asked to teach in a manner that can engage students and get results. Hence, I write this book. I do not profess that my way is the only way nor, certainly *the* right way, but rather that my way has proven, for me and others around me, to be a method that brings success with sanity. I, therefore, offer the following steps in the hope that you may find a strategy to employ from the very beginning that can bring you, hopefully, success in planning and teaching without overwhelming you. You, too, can be a good teacher and maintain your sanity!

❅❅❅❅❅

I teach high-school Spanish. I do not have training in any other discipline. I believe, however, that the basic steps that I suggest would work in most, if not all, subject-specific situations. In order to share what I have learned about successful curriculum implementation, I offer the seven steps I gave found have led me to success while maintaining most of my sanity: 1) play the hand you're dealt, 2) go toward the light, 3) pencil it in, 4) skim the cream from the top, 5) put the skeleton in the closet, 6) ...and the first shall be last and 7) notes to self...

Chapter 2

Step One: Ya' gotta play the hand you're dealt!

Step one just happened to me as it will happen to you, like it or not, ready or not. You start teaching at a school, you inherit the curriculum. We rarely have control of the curriculum we are required to implement, especially at the beginning of our careers or when we begin in a new school. So the hand you are dealt is the hand that you will have to play. Accept that there's usually no option but to hold 'em, you can't fold 'em or trade 'em in. States have state-wide standards. Districts have district-wide shared assessments. Schools have inter - departmental plans and/or goals, all of which are required, must be included and are often embedded in the curriculum.

Teachers usually have strong opinions about the content they are required to teach. This can be a very good thing, as the next time an opportunity arises to revise or rewrite the curriculum, they can speak up and make changes. But when beginning, the reality is usually that the lesson plans for next week or month or semester must reflect the content of the curriculum as it is envisaged to be implemented today.

All we learned in our education courses, clear objectives and learning targets, should be the focus of any curriculum, since mastery of those objectives is what should be assessed at the end of the course or at the end of units within the course. The first step, then, should be to peruse the written curriculum for evidence that the proposed content of the instruction is driven by the objectives. If your curriculum does not present the objectives up front (and many old ones may not), you will need to add a step zero: defining what you want students to learn (objectives and learning targets) before you can develop an overall plan for teaching and assessing. That's the subject of another book!

Okay. There are objectives. So what happens if the objectives are not clear? You will need to do a thorough exploration of the curriculum content and discern what the basic *essential* concepts, objectives and learning targets are (or should be) throughout the course. (Note the emphasis on essential! More about that later.) Having to add the step zero will, unfortunately, delay progress in the planning process more than if the curriculum you inherited had been solidly based on core objectives.

In some cases, the teacher new to the building may find that there is no written curriculum – a truly overwhelming discovery. When I first began teaching, a curriculum for Spanish (my subject) across the district did not exist. Each of our then 5 secondary schools could choose whichever book(s) they wanted to use – and there was only one teacher per language per building to make that decision. The school I (still) teach in had one book used for the first-year Spanish classes only. Levels two through five used a variety of resources, the greatest of which (I must say again) was the ingenuity of my student-teaching cooperating teacher, colleague and friend.

As I have said, I was very lucky. I was a student teacher in the same school the year before I was hired to teach there, and I had the opportunity to learn and begin to develop many of the strategies that I include here from my cooperating teacher. Without her knowledge, creativity and skill, I would likely have floundered , lost my sanity and given up in despair very early on in my career. Instead, I've lasted for more than 34 years because I, with early guidance and substantial trial and error, have sought methods of implementing curriculum in a way that works (not just for me, but for others, as well), produces results (students have returned from university to tell me that they are far more prepared than the others in their class) and, even more importantly, maintains my sanity in the process.

If you do find yourself without a curriculum, it will soon become evident that such a situation can be a double-edged sword. You can first rejoice in the freedom to design your own course from the ground up while simultaneously fretting about how you are going to figure out what to do and then do it in a way that ensures good teaching, leads to desired student achievement and doesn't drive you crazy. If you find yourself in this boat, as I did, you may find some solace in the fact that the following strategies will help with what you need. The difference between starting with a solid, workable, objective-based curriculum and having to create your own from scratch is that you will need to start with course design and curriculum development, a whole different ballgame from its implementation, and not the subject of this particular book.

✣✣✣✣✣

Once you know which cards have been dealt to you (hopefully in the form of essential outcomes or core objectives), it's time to move on to step two. Ready or not, there you go. You have the ingredients (and maybe the beginnings of a recipe). It's up to you to figure out how you will create an exceptional product.

Chapter 3
Step Two: Go toward the light!

Step two begins once the end result for which you are aiming has been identified in the official curriculum. The assessments that will be required throughout the course (or quarter, or trimester) must then be determined. Just like the light at the end of the tunnel may draw you toward it, the learning opportunities that you decide upon throughout the course must all be drawing students toward the planned summative assessment(s). I would suggest that the single most important concept of curriculum implementation is just this: backward planning. In other words, aim for the light at the end of that tunnel first, so you know where you are going and how you think you can get there in the most efficient and/or effective way; *then* plan, with that end of the tunnel as your focus.

In some situations, the written curriculum determines not only the final objectives but the summative activities to assess them, as well. In many cases, however, those assessments are left to the teacher to devise. Speaking of assessments, I must caution here that students tend to respond better to authentic assessments – things that they can do to show what they know *and can apply* in the real world and in school (Hiebert, Valencia & Afflerbach, 1994; Wiggins, 1993). Authentic assessment values the thinking behind the process of their work, as much as the finished product (Pearson & Valencia, 1987; Wiggins, 1989).

Rarely does the package with a purchased curriculum provide this type of assessment, as it is much more time consuming to prepare and to grade. Most textbooks include test banks, quizzes, workbooks and games, but not true authentic assessments. Authentic assessments of the same outcome may vary from school to school or district to district; the desired outcomes may be different from one teacher to another and/or the process to show what the student knows may be different; most teachers who want to be sure they are assessing authentically can plan to construct their own assessments rather than rely on the textbook that is made for the masses, not for one particular group of students.

Summative assessments should receive all of your attention at the beginning of the planning process (and, once again, is the subject for another book), superseded only by the previous determination of the essential outcomes or core objectives. You need to know where you are going before you can get there. You'd never think of driving away from your house with the intent to go to a particular party (the ultimate objective) without knowing where it was to occur. You'd never get to the party if you had no idea where you were going! Even knowing the address of where the party was, you would be hard pressed to arrive effortlessly and on time if you had no directions if the neighborhood were not familiar to you.   If you were familiar with the general neighborhood, you might get close enough to the party that you could hear it or someone could help you find it. However, if you had left your house with no idea of where you wanted to go other than "the party," chances are you would not even get close, much less arrive!

So why do teachers think that their students can arrive at that party (the summative assessment) without a planned route to direct them there, the originally-desired result? It wouldn't matter, either, if you were given several options for how to arrive; the end result (getting to the party with everyone else) would be accomplished. There may be several routes one might take to get to the party. Any twist or turn along the way might allow you to see or learn something that others didn't see or learn on their route, but eventually everyone would get to the party, the goal.

Continuing with the party metaphor, let's say that the party starts at 6:00, you are going to receive a special award in a short program before dinner at 6:30, and dinner will be served at 7:00. In most cases you, the recipient, would likely want to arrive at the party about the same time as other guests and certainly before award and dinner. To do so would require planning in advance, taking into account when to leave home and the best route to take to get you there at the appointed time with all of the other guests. If you were to not plan properly, others would arrive as the party gets going (from 6:00 to 7:00). You would not. While you would still be searching for the location, others would be ready to sit down to dinner together. And what about your award? If you arrive too late, you would miss receiving it at the designated place and time. The introduction would have been made, your name would have been called, everyone would have looked around for you – and you would be nowhere in sight!

If you had planned poorly or chosen a rather circuitous route, you might arrive once dinner has started. If you arrived during the appetizer, you may have simply saved yourself some extra calories, but your meal will most likely not be ruined. If you were to miss the full meal and arrive for dessert, however, you will have missed it, leaving you hungry and frustrated. It might be possible to grab something from the kitchen that was served for dinner, if available, but it wouldn't be as good and you may get only table scraps. And, finally, if you were to arrive at 9:00, you would have, finally, succeeded in arriving, but you will most likely be hungry, frustrated, unhappy, embarrassed and empty handed.

Let's translate that example into a class with students that is expected to arrive at a certain place at a specific time. It may be a time when students change classes or teachers. It may be the time for the summative assessment. It may simply be when others had previously agreed to arrive. If the teacher has not carefully considered the best route to lead the students to the assessment (with a detour or two, perhaps, according to the interests of the students or teacher), students will be missing what most other students are learning. They will be frustrated with the missing chunks. Some might be able to recoup their losses in the following classes (think getting there for some of the dinner); some may seek help outside of class to catch up (think table scraps); some students will never be exposed to the content they missed unless they do a lot of extra work to learn what they are missing or repeat the course.   And some will be frustrated, unhappy, embarrassed and empty handed as they forever have an information gap .

Back to the routing. Think of the time that could be wasted by taking a side street where something exciting is going on.   Students and teacher may become absorbed in something that, while interesting, does not lead to success on the summative assessment. This is not to say that teachers should not ever follow their own interests, those of the students or the opportunity for a teachable moment. The key point here is the danger of what can happen when there is no forethought involved in planning the route and arrival.

If you find yourself in a school in which you have colleagues teaching the same course, it is essential to collaborate! Planning is not a time to close your door and do your own thing! It doesn't help students if you hide from colleagues, not sharing ideas or products. (This would be the equivalent to driving from Minneapolis to New York by way of Los Angeles because that is what one person, the teacher, *you,* wants to do.)   While, ultimately, the learning encountered on the side may be valuable, it may not be the route you need to experience success on the final assessment. And, if you spend several hours wandering around without a particular focus, you may never even get to the assignment.

I found that our department grew stronger and provided better instruction when we began working together regularly in our Professional Learning Communities and our International Baccalaureate Middle Years Programme collaborative time. The more minds that work together, thinking, brainstorming and freely sharing, the better the results. In fact one of the greatest benefits of such collaboration could well be, as it has been for us, shared authentic summative assessments.   The purpose of collaborative planning is not to prescribe a day-to-day alignment, but rather to consider a general plan, in concert with others, that allows a students a chance to arrive at the same place with the same essential knowledge very close to the same time.

This concept forms the basis for the articulation mentioned earlier. Students will benefit from the planning that allows everyone the same chance to be successful on summative assessments without missing chunks, without a lot of extra work on their part, and without the frustration or embarrassment that students would feel when changing teachers, unprepared, from one marking period to another.

To effectively measure the level of success the students experience in the learning of the content you teach, assessments should be in place *before* any lesson planning or learning opportunity decisions are made. In other words, you need to plan the party before you give it. This means that you shouldn't start filling out a calendar with plans until you have identified the essential outcomes, the manner in which they will be assessed and the assessments themselves. This, unfortunately, is not what traditionally happens. Teachers often pick up the curriculum that needs to be taught, the textbook or units that they want to teach, thinking the party has already been planned for them. Some curricula may be specific enough to do this but, in my experience, that is rarely the case. Textbook companies, although changing, rarely provide effective *authentic* assessment. They usually just give you the party favors or the decorations.

All of the instruction that will be outlined in your lesson plan book should be directly related to successful achievement on the final, or summative, assessment. Activities in the classroom should look like the assessment. Yes, this means that you will be "teaching to the test." Those have been "dirty words" for educators in the past because they are usually interpreted to mean teaching to national or state standardized tests with prescribed content taught in a boring manner. There may be a valid argument here. However, aligning your plans for how students will be evaluated and then teaching them the skills they need in order to be evaluated is, indeed, best practice, even though it may be considered teaching to the test (Bushweller, 1997).

Providing instruction and practice of necessary skills is what happens in sports all the time. The coach puts the team through a variety of exercises that improve endurance or general abilities to perform the skills necessary to win a game. The team practices regularly the very things that will be done in a game (shooting free throws, throwing a touchdown pass) and often there are scrimmages or pre-season games to go through the exact same thing that will happen when the game is played for real. Actors spend countless hours practicing, including final dress rehearsals. Musicians play and replay countless times the very piece of music they will perform in concert. And we expect this in sports and arts. How is it that we think the very basic education that a student requires to become a productive citizen should be treated differently? Imagine our surprise if we discovered that our basketball team was preparing for the tournament finals by learning ballet. The team may become exceptionally good at pirouettes, but I'm betting they wouldn't be the winning basketball team!

Any athlete/actor/musician would say that repeating the very thing that they will have to do in a high-stakes moment is vital! So why is it that teachers preparing their students for an assessment are not supposed to do the same thing? Why is it considered a bad thing if teachers want students to show what they know through the application of the very skills in the very situations for which they are being coached?

It seems we accept sports, drama and musical training much more readily than practicing for/teaching to the test because, in sports, we are expecting every player on the team to show us what s/he has learned over/through time in its final test (the game). Let me repeat that previous statement: *we are expecting every player on the team to show us what s/he has learned over/through time in its final test.* Does that sound like something we may have been told in education classes, standards-based grading and authentic assessment? Does not this describe the very job of a teacher as a coach?

Most of us are not in the area when the teams are being coached for the game, the blocking of a script occurs or the musician learns the intricate moves necessary to play a great piece. The number of times s/he had to throw free throws in practice or how much weight could be lifted for the endurance necessary for the game only matters to the extent that the players have mastered the skills needed to do well in the final game. (So much so, actually, that we are not surprised when a coach loses his/her job based on the performance of the team.) We don't watch the practice. We watch the game! Yet we fully expect the team to perform at a high level in each game; we presume good coaching = winning. Does it not make sense, then, that we would want to do the same in our classrooms as on the sports field or the stage: practice the very things in the very ways that we will need to be successful in the final test? We must make teaching for success on the assessment our main objective and create learning opportunities that provide for it.

Why do we think that a teacher's job should be different from that of a coach?   Teachers provide practice in the skills that will be necessary in the long run for the final assessment; how many free throws someone can shoot one particular day in one given environment does not equal that athlete's ability to give their all in a manner that has a chance to win the game. How a student can memorize x bits of knowledge on one given day and spit them back out on another in a specific environment does not equate to a fair appraisal of the skills learned that provide the student with what they need to give them a chance to 'win the game.' Teach to the test? Coach to win a game? Give a team a win for the number of free throws shot in practice? Assess the student for spelling the words that may or may not be needed to write the essay? Or assess the final essay for writing skill and content learned throughout the practice for the game?

About eight years ago, my colleagues and I began to revise the way we collaborated to plan and assess our students in Spanish and French in a manner that was not at all like our textbooks. We were convinced that, with the implementation of the International Baccalaureate Middle Years Programme (MYP) in our school, to be followed by the addition of the Diploma Programme (DP), we needed to take a serious look at the anticipated progress needed three and four years down the road as we planned how and what to teach for our students. Consequently, the new common assessments we have designed include conversational Spanish and French in real-life situations, writing for a real-life purpose and the reading of authentic materials.

Authentically assessing students was not new to us (world languages have traditionally had an inherent facility for it).   The new part for us was to determine and write the assessments, along with their rubrics, at the *beginning* of each unit. We then determined what we would have to do in our classes throughout the unit to be sure the students could be successful in their final "game" (conversation, essay or reading). We realized that we needed to give students those very same experiences throughout the unit, as though we were coaching basketball players for a basketball game.

Redesigning our assessments has been (and continues to be) a very challenging, time-consuming and sometimes frustrating project. We have not been significantly changing our expected outcomes nor the activities we've used to teach to them. However, the actual process of writing the assessment before walking in to the classroom to teach anything has taken some paradigm shifting, as well as forethought and planning.

Mary E Condon

The result of defining our exact goals, expectations and specific skills for our students *before* we planned our instructional efforts has significantly changed our approach in the classroom. The assessment drives the instruction; in other words, the activities and tasks we plan now mimic the same knowledge and skills that the students will be required to produce for the summative assessment. We've broken skills and content into comprehensible chunks, as a coach would do: teach individual bits to be put together to play a good game at the end.

This does not mean the students practice THE actual test. Students are given the content and tools they will need to do well on the evaluative activity (as in basketball, drama or music). Depending on the skill we are trying to assess, the activities may exactly mimic those on the test or, at a higher level, will provide the students the chance to really show what they know through the application of the skills and content in a similar yet different situation, such as playing a different opponent in the basketball game, performing for those who hold differing opinions or expressing oneself through different media.

We actually have gone a step deeper. We knew that, ultimately, our students would be preparing for and taking the International Baccalaureate exams at the end of their senior year. We were given training early in the process about how to approach our MYP classes. However, we remained clueless about the eventual final the students would have. I insisted (repeatedly and often) to the Powers That Be that we could not start this journey without knowing where it was going to end. I knew that we were are all good teachers and could provide good teaching so our students could learn good Spanish and French. That was not the issue; we had been doing that for years. The issue was, rather, whether the students were going to be able to show what they knew in the IB DP way. Eventually I was allowed to attend the training that should have begun our journey. I was given access to the type of exams for which the students would sit. At that training we, the workshop participants, were given an assignment: set a timer and take the exam exactly as a DP student would. We did this to see just exactly we should be teaching our kids to be able to do to perform well on the IB test.

Wow! What an eye opener! The International Baccalaureate Diploma exam is structured very differently from the exams provided by textbook companies (the same is true of the AP exam, as well). While doing my "homework," I was pleased to see that the exams approached language learning in the same way I had been teaching for the previous 27 years. I have always wanted students to 'show what they know' in a culturally correct way before that ever became a catch phrase.

It immediately became clear to me after the first five minutes on the test, however, that a significant adjustment in my summative assessments (and the formative experiences leading to them) would be needed in order to teach my students to confidently approach the DP exam itself. Those who teach Advanced Placement (AP) courses have shared with me the opinion that the specific skill set necessary to do well on the final exam must be acquired, as well, in addition to demonstrating proficiency in the Spanish language. That proof of proficiency can be significantly different in the DP, AP or textbook.

My colleagues and I have been teaching so that our students might become proficient in the language. Within the first five minutes of taking the test it became very clear: we need to teach to the test! Not the content. We need to be sure that the *skills* have been acquired to demonstrate proficiency using whichever particular programme's assessment. In other words, we need to prepare them to perform well in the specific way the assessment requires.

Teaching a language has, as its ultimate goal, the creation of a proficient, bilingual person. Clearly, then, the test for proficiency should be the ability to function in a bilingual situation. There are several ways to demonstrate competence, at least the AP, DP and textbook way. We were convinced that if we continued to teach Spanish in the same manner in which we had been teaching and assessing, we would not be preparing our students for the eventual manner in which they would demonstrate mastery of the concept. Taking that DP exam ourselves (the same test students would take six years later) showed us that something in our instruction would have to change.

That DP test proved to be very challenging and somewhat intimidating, not because we didn't know the Spanish and French necessary, but because the assessments are written in a way that is very different. We'd been successfully teaching Spanish and French for years, but we had never approached it the DP way. We knew that, If we were to continue to teach as our past practice, we would give students Spanish and French knowledge, but they would know how to pirouette instead of play the basketball game.

As a result of our experience with that DP test, we immediately re-wrote our summative assessments and began to incorporate different formative experiences into our instruction (this seems to be a never-ending process, as well!). We did not change *what* we assess, we changed *how* we assess. We now provide activities that actually do mimic the eventual assessment; students practice the skills and knowledge by doing what they will need to do in the end: shoot a free throw in a game/hold a conversation at a given level of proficiency.

In the beginning, students were somewhat surprised when they learned that our formative activities prepare them for the very manner in which they will show what they know in the summative. They had not experienced this in other classes. I would argue that it is a little easier for us, as the handy thing about a language is no two conversations will ever be the same, so we give away nothing by practicing the very thing students will need to do.

As a side note, I found it interesting that our colleagues in our feeder schools were reluctant to take the DP test in order to see where their kids would be going when they left their school and went on to DP. They, in fact, refused all attempts of pressure by our school, our administration and the District Curriculum Coordinator. The result has been an even wider gap in skills than had existed previously. We surmised that those teachers were intimidated by the test or didn't believe that it could be really as different as we said it was. Furthermore, the other colleagues in other buildings continue, even now, to be more concerned about content than skill (what vs. how). The path down which we are moving with IB allowed us to see very clearly the difference between the two. The different emphasis on assessment is the primary reason that I was motivated to share our success with others.

Our expectations and level of rigor have increased considerably. At first, we were worried that students might struggle with the bar raised a little higher. We were astounded to learn that the students rose up to that bar, seemingly effortlessly. I know. It sounds too good to be true. We thought so, too. We were truly shocked at how well the students performed on the first (and subsequent) assessments given with our new plan for instruction (final rubric first, bits of skills in pieces to be put together and lots of practice – just like the athletes).

I do have to admit that this exact procedure may not work so well in other disciplines where there is a right and wrong process to reach a right or wrong answer. However, it seems to me that practice in the manner in which you learn to kick a ball, measure flour, analyze a poem, debate an amendment, play the flute, determine the amount of carpet to buy for a room, balance the books or prove an hypothesis could work the same way. It takes a shift in the way of thinking or of interpreting what is meant by "showing what you know."

Whew! This sounds like a lot of work. It is! We found, however, that by creating assessments before the teaching even begins, teachers know precisely how to plan activities so we really are teaching what will be evaluated in the manner in which it will be evaluated.

Too often teachers write the test after teaching the content, a day or two before the test. Or, worse, they use a book test that they have not looked through to be sure the content was taught. (Remember some of your college tests? You had to guess what the teacher might decide to include – the information from the book, the information from class, a combination of the two, or did s/he expect you to read his/her mind?) Many of those tests seemed to be about content, not skill. I would argue that if specific content needs to be assessed (think rules of basketball), the content should not be a surprise to the students as they sit to take the test!

And, if a skill is to be assessed (think free throw), it should not be assessed by spewing forth content or theory (the rules of the game).

I'm all about not thinking too much or working too hard. But I have learned through the years that in teaching, as in painting a house or planting a garden, if you do the preparation up front, have the right tools and know how to use them (or to find someone who does), the job is not only easier, it is more successful. I used to try to take shortcuts in the painting and planting, usually resulting from not having the right equipment. Paint and plants are things. When teaching students, we impact the lives of the future of our country. The stakes are much higher in school than in my housework. I have seen the results of the painting, the planting and the teaching without the proper preparation and tools – and it is not pretty. So if I can do something now that I'm going to have to do later anyway and it will allow me to end up with better results to boot, I'm going to ensure that the assessments I prepare for students will show real learning and are written *before* I begin the instruction.

It is important to note here that we have not changed our entire Spanish and French programs. So, once we had what we needed (map) to know where to go (party), we just needed bravery to attempt the plan. The rewards for that bravery have been better results (the game). In fact, our Language B classes scored, in total, higher than the international average on the first DP tests ever given in our programme.

Some teachers may be put off by the idea of determining the assessment and constructing their course around it because they have specific content that they want to include, no matter the objectives or assessment. These teachers need gentle guidance to align their enthusiasm for content and the curriculum material they are required to assess. It is usually possible to tweak content or instructional activity in some way if it relates to the topic. We have not changed our Spanish and French programs; we have, instead, realigned and planned ahead. We are experiencing phenomenal results while keeping our sanity.

Conversely, unfortunately, there are a couple of departments within the school that have clearly not planned assessments ahead. We have a calendar that DP teachers are expected to use in order to save our students from inundations of exams and other assessments in all six of their classes. There is one particular exam for which the teacher expressed, from the beginning, the need to continue to teach new things to the students right up until the international final assessment. I have heard this for three years now, and can't figure out why the teacher(s) cannot seem too plan a bit better. They have a curriculum, they have a book to use in their classes, they have calendars and they have had training. In my opinion, there can be no excuse for not planning well enough for the essential topics, tests and assessments needed over two full school years!

In chapter one, I listed some of the pitfalls of poor teacher planning that fails students (numbers one and four). I have heard the teacher(s) blame the IB exams, the textbook and the students for the difficulty they have in planning so all teaching is done (and well) by its required time. I suspect they are 1) not going toward the light and 2) not skimming the cream from the crop (see chapter 4) and blaming other sources rather than their own lack of appropriate planning. We should not be surprised, and should not fully blame the teacher. In the introduction, I mentioned that few teachers are ever taught to look at teaching, learning and assessing in this manner, neither from a supervising or cooperative teacher during the student teaching experience, nor from the principals and colleagues in the school where they land a job. Teachers can go their entire career without figuring out effective strategies for planning and assessing that could keep them sane!

In my experience, teachers generally become excited to see the success they experience when their assessments are genuinely aligned with the content and skills (actually, it's the other way around, but those teachers who were concerned about constructing the assessment before the instruction may not see it that way.) If only we could convince all the others out there to think of this as best practice, and not bad teaching!

I am very proud that the Language B classes in my school have been making big strides in planning by first determining the desired outcomes and then proceeding so students are prepared to show achievement of them. We are thrilled that our first ever DP exams showed our students to be quite a bit more proficient than the world average. For us, that was the best final assessment of success of our planning and instructional methods.

✤✤✤✤✤

Thus far, we assume a given curriculum (with essential outcomes) and assessments that will show us how well the students have learned the essential skills and content. We have now arrived at the point in the process when we begin the actual planning for successful delivery of the curriculum – in other words, its implementation.

Chapter 4
Step Three: Pencil it in!

Finally! We have reached the point where we can start to do what college really taught us, as teachers, to do: plan and place the instructional opportunities that we will provide in order to move our students through the lessons for successful assessment. Please notice that this is step THREE, not step one! And you thought, from the title, that we should have arrived here a whole lot sooner, didn't you? If you can change your ways to make this step three instead of step one, I'm convinced you will find that this will help you maintain your sanity and be more effective teacher.

My first rule for planning instruction is to use a pencil!! Things will change!!! Some schools provide a special book for lesson planning and teachers are required to turn in a copy every one or two weeks. If this is your situation you will, of course, comply. However, be sure that you start with a *full* calendar for the grading period your school uses (semester, trimester, quarter or other term). This can be in a plan book, a calendar on the wall, a calendar on the computer, or any other type or place. I usually use the plan book provided by my school. I have always used it to plan, so it is second nature for me. Several of my colleagues, however, cannot figure out how it could work for them and have no idea how I use it. They prefer to use a regular calendar for one class at a time rather than this example that plans six hours at a time. It doesn't matter what you use, but I would suggest that you print out the calendar and complete this step in pencil, rather than type it in on the computer as you as you go. You are *sketching* out a very rough idea of your plans; you are not engraving them in stone (your job is to teach; you are not a stone engraver!)

Don't panic; you are not going to write every detail of what you are going to do day by day!! Step three is the step many teachers miss altogether because they make the mistake of assuming this step is lesson planning.

Step three is not about lesson planning or curriculum design. It is the step where you will attempt to see the big picture of where the course is going. In other words, you're planning the party, drawing the flight plan, or setting our ship's course; remembering that it is vital to know where you are going before you can plan to get there!

First, on the calendar or in the plan book, identify all of the student-contact days within the marking period. Pencil in (ok, you could use ink here!) the final assessment time/day. If other summative assessments or more formal formative assessments are to be given (you'll know this – they are already written, remember?) throughout the term, pencil those in. (If you usually give those kinds of assessments on Friday, then pencil them in on Fridays.)

You will also probably want to include two or three interim assessments but cannot know exactly when they will fall, as the students need to learn and practice the content and skills first. What I have done (and insisted that my student teachers and new teachers I've mentored do – they do thank me later) is to write (in pencil!) across the top or in the margin of the week in which the assessment would best fit in order to appropriately space the assessments throughout the term.

Once you have a blank calendar of student-contact days (you'll see on the calendar where holidays may fall and the likely time you'll give summative assessments), you should peruse all of the curriculum once again (I know, redundant and time consuming -- precisely why this step is so hard for teachers to do well; but necessary if you want to implement the curriculum in an effective manner).

Next, chop up the term into two, three or four big chunks (or units, if you prefer). I think about the various things that must be taught during the given timeframe, divide those into chunks, then place those chunks in light pencil around/over/by the amount of time that I think that I will need to complete them. For example, if I know that I have nine units of study that I will need to cover, I will begin by deciding if the units are of more or less the same size. If so, that means I have to cover about three units per trimester (my district's marking term). I often play around with the placement and length and placement of units a little so that I can try to make them fit neatly into the calendar. Next, divide the year into marking periods (quarter, semester, trimester). Notice that you have not written ANYthing on the calendar yet other than the name of the "chunks." No lessons; not yet!

Using the nine-chunk scenario, I will need to teach three units in the first term, if they are of more or less comparable length. If they are not, I need to make the decision to move things around in some way. Assuming I want three units in a trimester of 12 weeks, I have approximately 4 weeks for each unit. Using my *pencil*, I then slice up the weeks into three equal weeks of four. If I know that unit two is short and unit three needs more time, I may pencil in two weeks for one and six weeks for the other. As I teach the units, I may find that my guess as to how much time I will need is not accurate. This is precisely why you are jotting with a *pencil*.

This part of step three is the most important, especially when you first attempt backward planning. And remember, until this point you have not yet written any lesson plans or ideas for activities! What you have done, however, is to establish exactly what it is that you want or need to teach throughout the term and/or year.

You already know how you are going to assess the students in a way that will allow them to show you what they have learned in authentic, practical context. And you know the approximate parameters of time that you will have to fit activities into the instruction. This gives you a place to start that assures you will arrive at the designated endpoint (the party) with everyone else.

I have found that teachers do not go usually go through this process, either because it has never been suggested or explained to them or because they begin here at my step three rather than my step one. Instead, they attempt to plan from the beginning. When that happens, teachers often don't allow themselves adequate parameters of time. Consequently, they will have to skip an entire unit or parts thereof (think back to arriving at the party after dinner). That is why they will they end up "behind" you (or you end up behind them). You could look at it this way: forward planning = falling behind!

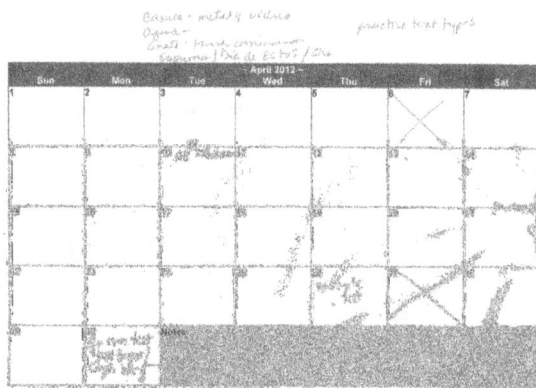

I want to be clear. This process is not the curriculum *writing* process; it is the *implementation* process. The curriculum is the shared tool for all teachers to bring their students to the final achievement point – we started with the assumption that such a document already exists along with already-created assessments.

The implementation is going to make or break student success and teacher sanity. Each teacher needs to take the responsibility of following this step, either alone or with collaboration with colleagues.

Collaboration at this point is extremely important if there is anyone else teaching the same course. Students do not have to (and probably should not) do the same things in the same ways on the same days in my class and in yours. But all teachers of the same course should generally be built around essential concepts, covering the same basic curricular material more or less within the same time parameters that have been determined in this step. This is particularly true if they are planning to give shared assessments. Thinking about the party, if I have an address and a route planned, I will show up at the party even if I take a different route (you just have to be planning to go to the same party as I!)

This leads to yet another issue. Many teachers truly do not know *how* to plan what they want to teach given content and time parameters. This piece is usually not taught to future educators – this is unit planning, not the lesson planning that is usually practiced in student teaching programs.

Here is a case in point. We had an experienced Spanish teacher join our faculty for a two-hour assignment one year. We showed her our curriculum (and where to find it) and the final assessments the other three of us were using. We told her to go ahead and teach anything in any way she wanted, as long as she was moving students toward success on the shared assessments. We also provided the collaborative products (ingredients) that were already created, as well as the recipe for their use, so she would have a place to start in her planning.

While an experienced teacher, she is connected to the textbook at her hip. For many weeks each of us tried in every way we could to explain and demonstrate what we meant by "achieve success on this assessment in whatever manner you wish." She saw two choices: follow the textbook (which the rest of us were not doing) or use our collaborative products (which needed explanation because she was not a part of writing them and didn't know what to do with them – remember the discussion of the flour and egg?).

Since our plans for second-year Spanish did not follow the textbook exactly, she felt that she was being trapped into using our specific plans. And right there is where all communication broke down! Her previous teaching experience was to teach pages 1 to 252 in the text, using the texts' ancillaries and tests. She was not accustomed to the freedom from the book that collaborative planning had brought to us. She resisted and then fled the teaching assignment at our school as fast as she could.

Ironically, her successor had much less experience and that experience had been in a very chaotic school environment. When my department worked with her to show her how we have developed our curriculum, she was immediately on board. She has been much happier in our building with our system. She transitioned easily to "our" way of doing things. It made sense to her, she tried it, she liked it. We filled the gap that many young teachers encounter without even knowing it. The sad part about that gap is that most teachers and principals are not even aware that this gap is often the primary source of the frustration many teachers experience. Being unaware, the veteran teachers and principals are unable to help close the gap. College courses do their job – they provide knowledge of content and classroom teaching skills, but it is a rare program that indoctrinates its students with full-fledged term-long planning for effective curriculum implementation. No one has ever shown them how to avoid the consequences of arriving late to the 'party.'

I think, perhaps, that principals presume that teachers should/be able to figure out the implementation on their own. Most don't. Or cannot. Or don't want to. Or won't. Those teachers are unaware of the possibility for success with sanity! My hope is that sharing my seven steps will provide a method that shows *how* and *why* we can have the necessary control to effectively implement curriculum.

✻✻✻✻✻

You now know where you are going. You have a general idea of a route to take to get you there about the same time as others within a given time frame. You are now ready for step four, the step in which you will choose the actual route, with specific learning opportunities that you want for your students.

Chapter 5
Step Four: Skim the cream from the top!

Finally! We have arrived at the point where we can begin to determine exactly what we will do day-by-day to teach the content and skills identified in the curriculum! If you are reading and find that my step four is usually your step one or two, please stop. Put your planning aside for a while, back up, re-read the first four chapters and follow the suggestions in them. Choosing what to include (and often, more importantly, to exclude!) in the plans or on the calendar is the next step to success with sanity.

Throughout the many years I have mentored teachers, I have always encouraged (or insisted) on backward planning, even when they haven't seemed to get the hang of it through observation, instruction or experience.   It just seems so obvious to me that following the first three steps sets you up to know exactly what to teach in the classroom day to day. It's hard for me to understand why anyone would resist getting to step four by way of steps one through three. To state the obvious, day to day planning can be tedious, but essential. These four steps should be helping to make it a little easier and to be well prepared to produce lesson plans. For one lesson at a time. Or linked to form a unit. We usually are not prepared to do long-term planning as we chart our course. Following step four, the heart of curriculum implementation, should make the process of planning easier and a lot more effective for teaching and learning.

As you begin to choose which daily activities you are going to use in your classroom, I believe it is imperative that you know exactly *why* you do each and every thing that is in your plan. The very first day I am with a new student teacher there are three things I always say to them, the first of which is, "The single most important thing a teacher needs to know and be able to do well is to explain *why* you have done everything exactly as you have." This applies to the previous steps in implementing the curriculum, as well, but it is especially important for your day-by-day planning if you want successful instruction and learning while keeping your sanity.

The reason I give for always knowing why is that everyone will always have to give you credit for the way you have decided to approach an issue, teach a class or share your opinion. Others may disagree with you or think that there is a better/preferred way to do things; however, with a logically supported, stated reason for everything you do, your plan will be considered to have value. (This is not to say that you shouldn't work with others to find the very best plan that, maybe, isn't yours.) Consider the ideas of others as you would hope they would consider yours. Rarely is there one single right or wrong plan when it is anchored by sound reasoning. Through discussion of the reasons behind each plan or way of thinking, you are likely to understand and be understood. Such discussion will likely lead to better collaboration, which will lead to better instruction

I really don't know who, if anyone, gave me this advice originally, but I am convinced that this "knowing why" thing really works for me in teaching. I have applied this concept from the beginning of my teaching career and have concluded that knowing why is the single most important component not only in lesson planning but in successful and sane teaching, as well.

When I was a new young teacher, I was observed by one of my Assistant Principals. During my lesson (I remember this as if it were yesterday and, again, I don't know why) there were three girls whispering to each other in the back right of the classroom. The AP was behind them and could observe the entire class fully engaged with the exception of those three girls. Later, in the debriefing session, the AP brought this to my attention and made suggestions for how (and why) I should have handled this differently, Without really thinking about it I thanked her for the advice and then explained that I had been fully aware of those girls and had made a conscious decision to ignore them. I did this because I knew, from prior conversations with them, that they were not really interested in learning Spanish; having them completely quiet would not have helped anyone else in the classroom to learn. The girls were quietly interacting among themselves without interfering with the lesson. I knew that if I were to make a scene or call them on their non-participation, they would have, based on past experience, become loud, sassy and disruptive.

The AP was surprised by my response. Even if one were to hold a different opinion, it would be hard to say that one is exactly right and one is completely wrong. (Of course, experienced advice is always worthy – or why would I be writing this book?) If one always knows why one is doing something and can articulate the reason, it has an amazing effect on the students, your colleagues, your superiors and parents. (And has, on more than one occasion, helped me out of a tight spot!) Student teachers usually take to this well, since they receive constructive criticism nearly every day; they find it easier to have a reason they can support to feel more confident and effective. It also makes a great deal of difference in the classroom, as nothing is done off the top of the head or by the seat of the pants of the teacher.

New teachers often take to this advice for the same reason as student teachers. Experienced teachers, whether they have been successful in the classroom or not, often tend to deny the existence of any other than their own. But those teachers often cannot explain why they have made the choices that they have.

One quick word of caution here. Explaining a logical reason why should be based on previous knowledge, the result of researching, learning how others have handled like situations successfully or devised to be done in a specific way for a particular purpose. The explanation should not be defensive; there should be no 'yeah, but's in the discussion of your reasoning.

Knowing why you want to do everything you do in the classroom will allow you to choose the activities best suited for your expected outcomes. It amazes me how much teaching goes on without any rationale. My friend (who had spent several years teaching in my school before budget cuts sent her to the other school in our district) was quick to ask the "why" of several practices in the new building that were quite different from ours.

For example, the final two days at the end of each trimester are scheduled as final tests, much like college, with a longer period of about 1 hour, 45 minutes. Our high schools provide those long blocks of time for final tests. Most teachers give final tests (in my school it is expected, in my friend's school it is suggested). In our school, the language classes use this time for students to complete an oral and/or written exam.

At the other school, however, my friend's new colleagues have been showing a film during each of the finals periods every year for many years, long before she arrived. The first thing my friend did, upon learning of this practice, was to ask why the films were shown. Were they applicable to the content of the course at the end of the trimester? How did they assist the students to meet the essential outcomes? Or is it a simply a way to entertain students without active teaching and without accumulating a pile of finals to correct? Is it for the benefit of the students and the curriculum, or the teacher?

The answers she received surprised and infuriated her. There is no reason, really, other than the teachers wanted to not make extra work for themselves and showing a film allowed that to happen. The choice of films did not have anything to do with the course content and in more than one case, both my friend and I challenged the appropriateness of the chosen film with regard to the level of the students.

In defense of the movies,, her colleagues said that anything cultural at any time in a language class is pertinent and worthwhile. While I could possibly be convinced that a movie can always be worthwhile in a foreign language class, I would be compelled to insist on a sound explanation as to why that would be. Why that particular movie?. Why at that particular time?

Why in that particular level of instruction? What would be done to tie the culture of the film into the language class and help to meet the essential outcomes? Why should that activity serve the purpose of the final test as expected by our district? Why.........

Later, as this friend was teaching a Spanish IV course that I had written in which certain films were, actually, integral part of the class content, she discovered that students had already seen them in some of the other teachers' classes. I see many things wrong with this picture, but I will call attention only to the lack of knowing *why* everything done in the classroom was chosen for the specific time and place. Clearly, this creates a difficult situation for vertical articulation that may actually harm the overall, big-picture curriculum.

✤✤✤✤✤

But I digress. In this step, you must consider all of the learning opportunities available to you that will lead the students to success on assessments of the essential outcomes (yes, repetitive but critical). I usually begin somewhere other than my lesson plan book. I make a list of all the things that I have done before, that I would like to do, that others do, that the textbook suggests, that I find in ancillary materials and any ideas that pop into my head. Obviously, it is impossible to do every possible activity, so decisions need to be made. Therefore step four: skim the cream from the top.

You know which activities are really big hits with the students, fun for you and, most importantly, lead to fulfilling the essential outcomes. Start there. Look at the textbook; most teacher's editions have some really good suggestions for a variety of ways to incorporate the lesson material. DO NOT plan to do all thirty two exercises provided in the textbook (plus the workbook, plus the video...) The textbook didn't give you all of those suggestions so that you can plow through them one by one. Those suggestions are there to give you a box of tools. Only some of those tools are really the best for a given situation and time frame. To use another analogy, if you are doing household repairs, you choose from the toolbox what you need to get the job done. You wouldn't try to put in a screw in with a hammer, nor would you use a screwdriver to pound a nail (I know, I've been known to do it, too, in a pinch, but it doesn't work very well!). You would not use a tape measure to remove a nail from the wall. You would choose the particular tool that will work best for your particular case.

There is a large number of teachers out there who really think that they should teach pages 1 to 252, inclusive, because they have never thought of the text as a tool box from which to select, rather than the tool itself. This is most likely the problem with the IB class mentioned earlier in which the teacher believes that new instruction must continue up to the very day of the test.

Once again, when studying education in college, teachers are usually not trained in how to choose a textbook or how to use it. I would suggest that more time be spent on this as a part of learning to plan lessons. We must select the tools from the toolbox that would best get the job done. If we but looked at it in this way, would it not make sense to us? I don't believe that teachers plan to teach pages 1 to 252 because they are lazy and want the text to plan for them, nor because they are incompetent and need the text to plan for them. I would argue that teachers use all of the pages with all of the activities because no one has yet shown them another option that makes sense to them! Nor has anyone probably told them that to teach well, one must skim the cream from the top – not everything is best for every teacher in every classroom that buys the book.

Many years ago, another colleague who taught German asked my advice as to how she was going to manage to get all of the activities in the book completed in the time she had left before the end of the trimester. (No, she hadn't backward planned and didn't have essential outcomes she was chasing. She was just going chapter by chapter and exercise by exercise through the book!) Upon hearing her frustration, I asked her the question that to me was so clear: *Why* are you doing that? Which activities are really the good ones that help students learn. Wasn't she (and the students!) bored?

Her answer astounded me. No, she had never really thought about why. She had to "cover" certain chapters in the book, and that is the only way she knew into do that. This is was a teachable moment, for sure! I shared with her how good it feels to always know why each thing is done in a particular way in each class. It's not that she had been teaching badly, nor that she had not been taught how to teach well. She simply had never considered (nor received instruction for or the suggestion of) the need to ask herself why she does what she does in her classroom so that she could select the best tools to get the job done..

A favorite example that I often share for knowing why is that of is a past Spanish teacher who began his full-time career at our high school after having done his student teaching in another high school in our district. He expressed surprise at the way in which we began our Spanish I classes. The book that we used at that time used three chapters to teach the verb *ser*, "to be:" one chapter for the first and second person, then another with the third person plural and we forms, and finally a third with the third person singular and plural. The textbook was set up, as many foreign language-learning texts are , to spend three weeks on each chapter. That is nine week, just to say "I am, you are, he is!"

Since I have usually been the person who has decided what and how to teach in our building, we have never spent that kind of time on one verb and its companying vocabulary! As he was collaborating with the other Spanish I teachers, he shared that his collaborating teacher at the other school had followed the textbook exactly as it was "supposed" to be done. I was incredulous! It was hard to believe that someone experienced in language teaching would take so long to teach what was presented in the book without choosing to adapt. Nine weeks!! That is almost 3/4 of a trimester following the textbook. Nine weeks!! There is much too much to do spend that kind of time on one verb (granted, there were new concepts and vocabulary that accompanied it but, really... NINE weeks?)!

Our Spanish I teachers shared with this colleague how we have done it at our school (for as long as I have been there). He was astounded at the concept of choosing and adapting, but immediately embraced it. He said he had taught at the other school just as his cooperating teacher had. He never given a thought to looking at another way to use the book and teach the concepts (not surprising, as this was his first real opportunity to teach). He learned that it is more liberating to do what seems best pedagogically for him and his students, rather than blindly teaching one chapter after the other following the guidance of the publisher. He expressed to me on more than one occasion how good it felt to be able to teach in a way that really makes sense. And, of course, he now agrees that nine weeks for "to be" is ridiculous – no matter the textbook.

Many new teachers are overwhelmed and follow the textbook pages 1 through 252 because it is the easiest route for them. I understand that the vast majority of teachers don't think the way I do – but I have experienced such success in the classroom with students who are interested in learning who are challenged and excited about learning at an appropriate pace for them.

Again, I don't know where, exactly, my method of planning and implementation originated. It has always just seemed so natural to me to manipulate the things that are necessary to learn to provide the best experience for the students. I've never been worried about having all the ancillary materials that would do that for me. The publisher doesn't know this class this year. I'm convinced that the publisher does not intend for all teachers to teach all 252 pages straight through following their suggested lesson plan, either.

I mentioned at the beginning of this chapter that this method of implementing curriculum has gotten me into 'trouble' with colleagues at the other schools. I should explain that, at this time, remains only me and one other teacher who began in the days when there weren't shared textbooks. She has always taught at the junior high and has only taught Spanish I and II. This means that, as I have tried to work with others in the district, there have always been comments (not all flattering) about the way that "*Mary* does it: she doesn't use a textbook." This attitude (from lack of knowledge of how this really can work) has made it very challenging for me to share my philosophy with other colleagues in my district an effective way to plan and implement curriculum without a book while providing high-caliber instruction and exciting and engaging opportunities for my students.

I have spent most of my career as the Department Chairperson of the World Language Department (this is *not* a role of authority nor power; it means I get to sit through long meetings, break news to my department of changes they won't like, and get paid about three cents per day for the privilege). As Chair, I have had an opportunity to mentor most of the Language teachers in my building as they have come and gone. All of them soon learn that I will be asking them to be able to share *why* they are choosing each thing they do in the classroom. This shared understanding of purpose has created a department that is one of the strongest in the building, as well as one of the most progressive. And now, teachers who join us find out what we are doing and how we do it and quickly learn to do it themselves, for they immediately see the success it brings.

Many new teachers are overwhelmed and follow the textbook pages 1 through 252 because it is the easiest route for them. I would argue that following the previous steps one to four is actually an easier route. At least in the classroom with students who should be interested in learning, challenged and excited about learning. I have found that the only way to stay sane while basing instruction on a textbook and its ancillaries is to skim the cream from the top.

✿✿✿✿✿

And now, about that textbook....

Chapter 6
Step Five: Put the skeleton in the closet!

Step five. Wow. Interestingly, this step has caused me a lot of grief for the past thirty four years with colleagues, parents and students. What is the skeleton? It's the textbook. The prescription, according to many, for the course.

I truly believe, however, that no publisher actually believes that teachers will try to teach everything as written or do every single activity in the textbook. The textbook is a guide with a lot of ideas, a skeleton for the framework of the course. Publishers dress the skeleton well, as they know that teachers look to the text to determine the course curriculum for them. Many teachers don't realize that one size does not always fit all; they should dress the skeleton according to the needs of the specific situation – changing its clothes for the best fit for the specific course, perhaps even stripping its clothes completely if and when it becomes necessary.

Given the time constraints, difference in classes from hour to hour or year to year, there is no way to successfully include everything the text provides. It is for this reason that I suggest that, after you have sucked all the life out of the skeleton, put it back in the closet!

That's not to say that you shouldn't ever take the book out of the closet again. It is to say that you shouldn't have to give one book to every student who will then feel obligated to haul it back and forth from school to home. Instead, build your plans around those good ideas from the book and your best ideas, and the best idea of your colleagues. Only pull the books out when you really need them. Students will thank you! It's one less book in their bag. It's one less thing to have to remember or forget. It's one less thing that represents boring bookwork. And with today's technology, most textbooks have some sort of online textbook and/or workbook, should you still feel the need to be assigning a large amount of exercises from it.

If you agree that the order in which the textbook progresses is pedagogically sound, the book can serve as the perfect skeleton as is. That means that you may follow the direction of the book, teaching the core content in the order presented but without using all of the activities (see step four). This has always just seemed best practice to me. I started teaching with a textbook that was different from every other school; that book was for one level of five Spanish levels taught in the district's five secondary schools, and there was no district-wide curriculum.

As I mentioned previously, I was very lucky. I student taught in this situation with a cooperating teacher that had, as I suggest, used the textbook as a skeleton. OK, the reason was that the book really wasn't very interesting (anyone remember foreign language books in the '70s?) and she had found a variety of sources and tools to use. The reason doesn't really matter. She had expertly designed and taught courses that did not need one specific textbook (in days way before the internet). The first and only way I really learned to teach Spanish, I learned from her. I have no doubt that I learned from the best! I also have no doubt that I have maintained my sanity throughout all of the changes in theory, regulations and personnel that I have experienced in the past 34 years because of my student teaching experience. That experience also allowed me to view curriculum development and implementation through a different lens than most.

Back when I started, there was one teacher per language in our building: French, German and Spanish. It wasn't an era of collaboration, either. We were all friendly on a personal level, but never got together on a professional level to brainstorm how we could deliver the best instructional experience for our students. I built on the units bequeathed to me by my cooperating teacher when she left; it seemed the most natural thing in the world to me.

Our language program began to grow (there are a lot of reasons for this, the biggest being that universities swung the pendulum back to requiring that students have a certain proficiency level in language upon entering college). As another part-time, followed by a different full-time, followed by various other Spanish teachers were hired, I shared with them what I thought they should teach and, lacking a text, they were a little uncomfortable with planning daily lessons. They were, therefore, thankful for my leadership (and learned a new way to look at curriculum in the bargain).

In the early 1980s, our district went to a full textbook adoption and written curriculum across all schools teaching languages. Suddenly, we all had to talk to each other about what we had been doing in our building. Since we were going to adopt a textbook for each level of each language, we looked at all the possibilities out there. Most of the teachers in the other building wanted a self-contained textbook. In other words, a book with workbook, audio and video supplementary materials and quizzes and tests prepackaged with the text. They were looking for the perfect package that would allow them to teach only using the book, not using their creativity to build on the textbook. That process at the time felt, to me, more like confrontation than collaboration. And those feelings hang on.....on both sides.

I was (and am) not opposed to using a textbook. I was (and am) opposed to the idea that there should be one and only one resource (text) with the idea that we teach given content in a particular order on a particular day with everything done for us through the ancillary materials. We all need to know which party we are going to and how to get there. We need a good idea for the best route to take. But we don't have to let a textbook dictate everything down to where to park the car when we get there!

✽✽✽✽✽

The thing that really bother me is that other teachers haven't wanted to have to do all the work of lesson planning (this has been expressed verbally in no uncertain terms during some textbook selection meetings in the past). They have wanted to adopt a textbook that has everything ready-made for them, from lesson plans, to workbook pages to quizzes and tests. At least that's what they said; I can't believe they really want to give away any and all creativity in course design and teaching!

The second thing I always tell my student teachers is "the textbook is but a skeleton." The teacher needs to provide the flesh. No book could possibly provide the exact material that every teacher would think is important to cover in all classes with all students all of the time.

Here is a good example. The first year that one of the junior high teachers began teaching second-year Spanish, she went by the book. In other words, if the verbs or vocabulary were in the book, they were taught; if not, they were not taught. As we were sharing what we were doing in our classrooms one day, she was surprised that my students had been exposed to much more vocabulary than hers. This was due to a general list of regular verbs that were not in the textbook but that we use as a staple in our second-year classes . I explained to her that I had a list of a jillion regular verbs that I give to the students. While we review the conjugation of the regular verbs, we also increase our vocabulary (and avoid boredom) by reviewing the conjugation of other verbs that work the same way. All she said in surprised response to me was, "Gosh, I never thought of that." She had only been thinking of the textbook – if it is there, teach it; if not, don't.

As I was helping our French department rethink their curriculum in light of the IB MYP, I learned that one of my colleagues had been doing the same thing in her French classes for quite some time. There is a chapter in their text that deals with taking a cruise and the corresponding vocabulary that cruising entails. The school in which we teach has a large population of students on free and reduced lunch. Many of them would never even be able to consider taking a cruise. She believed that there were other things of more importance to teach in that chapter and in that term, so she dropped the cruise piece, teaching the other material in the chapter in a different way. This really bothered French teachers at other schools, since if it is in the textbook, it is the curriculum. And the curriculum must be taught. And therein lies the great divide.

Should a textbook be chosen and adopted and then the curriculum be written, or does one write the curriculum and find a textbook that will do the best job delivering it. I've found that most teachers believe it is the former. The book = the curriculum. But that would have to mean that the book's publisher is the determining factor in deciding what your students should learn and when, and how they should be assessed. Why would teachers want to give such power to a company they will never see? How would teachers justify that curriculum if it didn't mesh with district, state or national standards?

Our district is supposed to follow a very established seven-year curriculum adoption process. I believe that this process is not named correctly; it's a textbook adoption process (nor has it really been only seven years!). Do we really want to re-write *curriculum* every time we change textbooks? Do we really think that the essential outcomes for learning a foreign language as a second language should change every seven years? Do we think that reinventing the wheel every so often is less work or gets better results? I would hope not!

When I was a new, young teacher in the district at the bottom of the totem pole, I was adamant in curriculum writing that we should establish what we want the students to know without listing each and every thing specifically and call that curriculum. In other words, the written curriculum should be what is *essential* that our students know at the end of each year (or term). The textbook can then assist us, lend us a hand, hold us up as we taught these things. In other words, the textbook is the skeleton; what we specifically want students to know is the flesh. I was an anomaly, however, but we did generally find a way to compromise by being only somewhat specific while leaving the door open to individual choice.

Another of my previous favorite student teachers and current colleague, Sara, uses a different analogy than the skeleton (she thought she'd gotten it from me, but she didn't). She says that the textbook is the ship. The ship needs crew to control its movements. The ship has no say in the kind of weather or water conditions it might encounter. The passengers rely on the crew to maneuver the ship through any and everything in a manner that will get them safely and efficiently to their destination. (I wish I *would* have said that!) The textbook is the ship. It cannot get from point A to point B by itself. And it can't always take the same path due to the way the winds blow in the field of education. But do the essential concepts for the class float around? We can only hope not.

I have continued to share my strong feelings on this with teachers, curriculum specialists and administrators throughout my tenure. I've experienced a lot of opposition, especially from colleagues who do not teach in my building. The most memorable example was a textbook adoption that was made with a new Curriculum Director. Unfortunately, that position had (and still has) the responsibility for all years of English, Reading, and World Language instruction. I won't even comment on how much sense that makes.....or not. She was unfamiliar with languages other than English, but she knew that you picked out a textbook you liked and then wrote the curriculum to teach. That was where she was coming from as a curriculum specialist! She was really frustrated with the Spanish teachers in our building who insisted on writing the *definitive* curriculum first, and *then* looking for the textbook most closely aligned with it that would serve us best (as a skeleton).

Please understand that I don't believe that curriculum, standards, or expectations will never change. Of course they will (and should, if and when necessary; sometimes more frequently in some areas, perhaps, other than in Spanish or French). However, the curriculum changes themselves should be rewritten as necessary to meet the demands of any new research, theory or standards, expectations or major changes in methods of instruction (such as, for us, the transition to the IB MYP).

It is also important, when writing the curriculum, that the essential concepts drive it (have I mentioned this yet?). It behooves us to be careful with this, though, as this whole essential concept/curriculum thing can go way too far into detail. I was once working on a district-level essential outcomes committee and, when someone started by suggesting that the alphabet is something all students should know at the beginning, a full 3/4 hour (I kid you not – I was timing it!) discussion ensued: What do you mean by alphabet? Should they know how to say it, how to spell with it, how the letters sound…It can be taught in one hour and then you're done – is that an essential concept?

Puhhhh-leeeaase. In a language, students should be able to know and use the alphabet. Do kindergarten teachers decide exactly what is meant by 'know the alphabet?' (I also have an elementary education degree, and am familiar with curriculum and its delivery, although I have never taught that level.) Things may have changed, but I don't recall asking for (or wanting) the specific, exact, spelled-out definition of what the alphabet is and if, when and how it should be taught. There are innumerable ways in which to practice a concept such the alphabet, in the classroom. The ways in which a teacher choses to work with the concepts in different ways throughout the instructional activities is, actually, the *implementation* of the curriculum. An essential concept is rarely a one and done lesson.

But I digress yet again. Back to the original story – writing a curriculum to choose a text or choose a text to write the curriculum. The Spanish teachers did, indeed, write a curriculum before searching for a textbook. This was (and is, I believe) the generally-accepted best practice for curriculum development. The French and German teachers, however, chose a new text and then wrote the curriculum, apparently planning to teach all of the pages from 1 to 252. With this approach, the curriculum they wrote will have to be rewritten years later with the adoption of every new textbook. The Spanish teachers, on the other hand, have been able to refer to their original curriculum writing (from 1978) when we need to produce new documents that match required format and best-practice theory. To me, that indicates that we know what we think really needs to be taught and that those concepts do not change, no matter how the texts may change. The text just assists us in planning a route to the party.

✤✤✤✤✤

Before I leave this step that I believe to be the single most important concept of this book, I want to address how one can successfully use the textbook as a skeleton.

As I said earlier, skim the cream from the top. I have sat several hours at different times with the teacher edition, paging through it (usually while I am relaxing by watching television in the evening – so it doesn't really seem like 'work'). I read all of the suggestions the book gives for in- and out-of-class activities. There are always some great ideas and, something that surprises me, even new ideas after all these years. I make a list of the activities and the content or exercises that I think do the best job for the concept. I then look in other books, or in my notes from a workshop, or consider the ideas of my colleagues that are new to me until I am satisfied that I have more than enough to use in my classroom during the time I have.

Next, I think about how the content and activities would make the most sense together; this provides the basis for what I pencil in on my planning calendar. Finally, I gather all of my resources and develop them or make them ready for use in the classroom. I usually use the textbook itself about 10% of my total teaching time – for most of my ideas about how to use the material, I'm leaning on the textbook. In other words I, as the teacher, really do use the textbook. But not for teaching. For planning.

Chapter 7
Step Six: ...and the first shall be last...

We've done it! We have now finally arrived at the point where you actually fill in the plan book and write the lesson plans! We can finally start at the beginning of the plan book. This is where I first write in ink – if I'm pretty sure that I have a handle on how much time I will need for the activities I've chosen – otherwise I stay with pencil.   And this year, with five different class preparations, two of them completely new, it seems that I have resorted to stickie notes so I can change my mind and my plans more easily. You may be surprised that I wait until last to do what most people usually do first. You need to remember that over the past 34 years, I have watched more teachers than I can count suffer anxiety and/or deliver less-than-effective teaching, even when they are good teachers.   The planning (or lack thereof) by looking at the end first and the beginning last is the key. All of the groundwork needs to be laid before successful lesson plans can be written. To my recollection, this was never taught to me in college and, if I can judge from recent student teachers, this is still not taught today. I know that the words "backward planning" are out there, but I also know that this terminology can sometimes be confused with the specific framework referred to as Backward Design© (Wiggins & McTighe, 2001) and just because the words are out there does not mean that this is a skill that is taught to, practiced by or mastered by student teachers. And then, of course, there are those teachers who have taught their own personal way for the last several years, unaware that there may be a better planning strategy out there that may work better for them.

At this point, we presume that we have a curriculum driven by essential outcomes, we have mapped out a rough schedule for our marking period or teaching unit and have chosen the activities that will be the most engaging for the students and give them the best chance for a good performance on the authentic assessment. Everything is now ready, except to place all of the various activities that we have decided that we want to use into day – by - day lesson plans.

I usually try to lay out at least one full week at a time when I finally arrive at the forward-planning stage.

One day at a time just doesn't seem to give me enough of the entire picture and often gets me stuck in spending too little or too much time on a particular lesson. Even though I am forward planning at this point (meaning that I am at the front of the plan book instead of the end), I am still applying the backward-planning concept to the week at hand. There are several situations in which teachers find themselves new to this kind of planning: a student teacher or new teacher who is inventing the wheel for the first time (or relying on a textbook or colleague to take them by the hand); the teacher who has taught for a while and knows the timing and probable success of the lesson plans s/he has used in the past, and the veteran teacher who is either trying out this backward planning thing for the first time or is beginning to teach a new course or implementing a new textbook.

First, let's look at the student teacher or beginning teacher. Rachel, the student teacher I mentioned previously, had a really hard time giving me even a full week's plan ahead of her teaching; she went day to day in her planning until her very last day with me. I understand that the first time through teaching something and developing learning opportunities for instruction and practice, the teacher may not have any real idea of how much time to allow for each activity, so they may think that planning day to day as they go makes more sense. My experience has shown that to not be case. By looking at the week as a whole, considering where a logical break would be for the weekend or when it would or would not make sense to begin a new concept on Friday, more coherent plans are possible. New teachers are either required to produce lesson plans or feel quite comfortable when doing so, as lesson plans are usually what colleges excel at teaching and requiring of teachers. This usually means lesson plans that are, by nature, isolated bits of teaching planned for one or two days. It would be a shame to come this far in the concept of backward planning and then throw it out as we plan for each week. The teacher must determine what the light at the end of the week's tunnel is and then draw the students to it in a practical manner. If this does not occur, teachers will continue to end up "short" or "behind" the original benchmarks because they will be, again, planning from the front rather than the end.

Second, let's consider the veteran teacher who tries backward planning with lessons that s/he is used to teaching. This set of teachers is probably the best group with which to hop on the backward-planning bandwagon. Those teachers are aware of the lessons they want to teach, how they are usually received by students and how much time they usually take. Armed with that knowledge, the teacher has a better sense of how the activities that they skimmed off the top in step four would work together and flow throughout a week. This group of teachers will not experience a steep learning curve when they continue the backward-planning concept through week-long plans. They are better able to assess whether the activity will fill a class period or go over its time and whether it would be better or worse to begin or end the unit on any given day.

The veteran teacher who is teaching a new course or using a new textbook for the first time will probably find the backward-planning process to be easier than it is for new teachers. Once we have some experience under our belt, we have a feel for what we believe students need to know about the topic we teach and we have an idea of the activities best equipped to teach it. In this case, the teacher needs to be very careful to avoid the day-by-day trap. I've been there, done that. I've pulled lessons out of thin air as I've walked into the classroom. I've changed the lesson in midstream if a better idea came to me. And I've even taught a lesson I had not read or worked with ahead of time. Sometimes that works. Sometimes it is actually better. But usually it is really not a good thing! Not for me, nor the students, nor for my self-esteem or effectiveness as a teacher. That lack of self-esteem is most likely what motivated me early on to do this planning-ahead-by-backward-planning system that I have used throughout my career. Implementing new instruction at any point in the term should require that a teacher follow the steps for backward planning not only for the term, but for the unit and the week, as well.   You still aren't going to get to that party you planned to attend a while ago if you don't have directions – today, next week or next term. I usually find myself applying the backward-planning steps each week and, yes, even for daily lesson plans. If you know you have 55 minutes to teach and practice something, you can do something differently than if you have 45 minutes.   Variations in class schedules are usually not, but may be, a surprise at the beginning of the school day. Those variations need to be considered as an important part of the planning process.

Finally, the veteran teacher who is learning to apply backward planning for the first time should find it easier than others do, as long as s/he approaches this idea with an open mind and is willing to let go of the way s/he has done things for the past several years. It can come fairly easily to those who know what they want to teach, how they want to teach it and have solid, proven lesson plans going in. It should come somewhat easily to those teachers who have taught the content in the past and can rely on their previous lesson plans. I must caution here, however, that the mind has to open a little to the possibility of giving up some things that have been done on a certain day, in a certain way in the past. This teacher needs to review step four and be sure to skim the cream from the top. It is quite possible that there is an alternative (and perhaps better) way to teach the material with which s/he is familiar. Accepting that can be difficult for those who are used to the way that things have always been done and don't really want to consider any other way.

✤✤✤✤✤

I have several authentic activities that I have developed for my advanced Spanish classes. These are cultural simulations that give the students the opportunity to *feel* the things I am teaching, not just hear or read about them. For example, I use a rich/poor simulation I've developed that requires substantial up-front preparation and requires at least one entire class period. I use a voting simulation based on my experiences in Latin America as an Official International Elections Observer in El Salvador, Guatemala, Nicaragua and Mexico. This simulation also needs substantial preparation and at least one full class hour to complete. I like to use the cultural simulation called Bafá Bafá (Simulation Training Systems, 2001-2011) with my class in combination with others. This takes planning between at least two teachers and requires at least two, sometimes three, class periods to complete and debrief. Not only do all of these require substantial pre-planning in order to set them up for my students, they also require careful planning so they occur after the appropriate previous instruction and will be uninterrupted by a weekend (for the debriefing to have its best value). I know I want to do these activities. I know about how much time to plan for each of them and when they fit best into my planned curriculum. All of them are time consuming, yet remain the most authentic experiences I can provide for my students. They are penciled in with assessments when I do my backward planning.

As I approach the week in which I have planned to include the simulation (these are undoubtedly among the cream from the top), I always have to reassess. Will this fit appropriately into the time I have left after "life" has happened while teaching the unit? Do I have time to do it right? Is there something else that could do it as well? Is there something else I could cut out so that I can include the simulation?

The answers always seem to be different. There are years when I have excluded a game such as Monopoly or Clue (very good activities for reviewing commands and the preterit/imperfect in Spanish), a film that is usually a part of the course or a simulation or two. It is with careful consideration that I do so, but to stay sane, I know that I cannot do it all every year. Classes are different, slower at some things, faster at others, interested in some things and not in others.   I, thankfully, came to terms with this early in my career (or I would not have kept my sanity!).   Plan, but be prepared to scrap the plans and go for plan B (or C or Z...)

The mistake of many is not considering the possibility of excluding their favorite or perceived indispensable activities. I have heard from teachers new to the backward-planning thing, "I have this unit that is so wonderful that I have always taught, how can I make fit it in?; but we *have* to show this movie during this unit; I'm going to be out of school those days (for a workshop, surgery, etc.) and I was thinking I would just throw in a movie...." Open mind, let go, plan backward before you plan from the beginning. Go toward the light at the end of the tunnel and allow it to draw you through to your ultimate destination!

Chapter 8
Step Seven: Notes to self....

It is important that all plans be continually reviewed, revised and rewritten. I often write notes in the plan book that say "next year do....." Or I use sticky notes to indicate things I would change the next time around. And, more recently, I've taken to keeping a second plan book with the reality of the class, vs. the planned version (the planned version never goes as I plan it); I change things day by day, week by week or even topic by topic in a different order that I have penciled in and written in ink. In fact, with the five preps I have, I seem to be moving things around more than usual. I have surpassed my past practice of cutting out a vertical sheet of the plan book to tape over the original to using sticky notes so that I can move the activities around. I am not really comfortable in my own skin with all of these new things to plan, but because I have honed my planning skills, I continue to be able to rely on them to keep my sanity.

Here is an example of how my plan book looked throughout the whole school year last year – and I only had *one* new course to teach then!

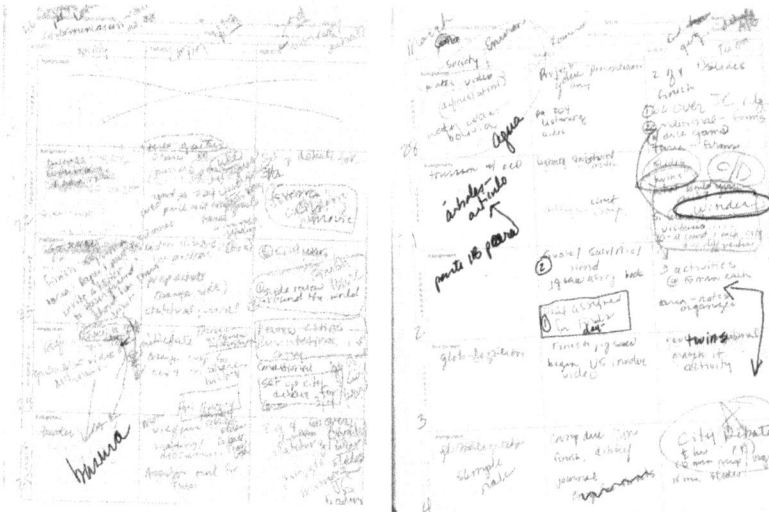

I know you can't really read the plans in this book. Don't worry, I couldn't read most of it last year even as I was teaching from it. It seems that I may be blowing my "pencil it in" all to pieces here, so let me explain.

If you look closely at the margins across the top, you will see the remnants of the first planning that I did at the very beginning of the school year. You will also see a sticky note and some planning notes, as well. And then there is the mess of writing on top of writing written over the writing. What you cannot tell in this photo is that the heavier lines were in different colors so I could keep track of my latest changes. It is not unusual for me to change my weekly plan day by day – the way most people write them. The difference is that I myself have set within some parameters that keep me on the straight and narrow whereas, if I were writing out the week for the first time as I moved forward, that would not be the case.

What I have done here is to create a comfortable and safe space for myself where all the major thinking and planning has already been done; I know where I am going and how I am going to get there. I just have to make adjustments with the pace and interest of the students. I think it would be much scarier to look at this plan book and see only Monday and Tuesday filled in, with the rest of the week blank and waiting to be filled. If that were the case, that would mean that now, right now before tomorrow, I would have to decide what I was going to do *tomorrow*, why I was going to do it, how I was going to do it, and I'd have to figure out what I would need in order to do that (oops, don't have the photocopies?), and feel as though I were running around like a crazy person. (That method is, truly, what

Rachel used during her entire time with me as a student teacher. It drove me crazy. It drove her crazy that I wanted her to look at the big picture and work backwards. When she became a colleague and was solely responsible for figuring out what she was going to do day by day, she agreed that planning ahead by backward planning is the only way to stay sane, given all the other things we need to do each day as teachers.)

Once she started, Rachel was hooked. She hadn't found a way to give me even one week's plan ahead of time when she was student teaching; the need to teach three different courses in two different languages in four different rooms each day did the trick!

I hope that by sharing some of the actual pages of my plan book with you that you will see I am not advocating hard and fast planning that is not flexible! Quite the contrary. By having the lessons planned (and the photo copies ordered!), I can relax and slide plans around with arrows. I usually have Plan B indicated in my plans, too , in case I misjudged and the activity uses less time than I had anticipated. However, when I 'over plan' with a plan B, I have no intention of forcing that plan into action – it's one of those things that would be good, interesting, engaging and helpful but extra, not essential.

For better or worse, my plan books have looked like this every year for the past 34. The more experienced I become, the more my plan book looks like this and becomes difficult to read. That is why I have, these last couple of years, begun to write a clean set of plans that to refer to later.

What I still find difficult to understand after all this time is how I can use the clean set from last year as the base for planning this year and my plan book always looks like this anyway (the example above was originally based on a clean set of plans from the previous year)! I do know that this illustrates how planning and teaching, even the same courses in more or less the same way, is never stagnant. That is precisely why I believe that I need to have a way to plan that, every time, regardless of the circumstances, allows me to successfully implement the curriculum while staying sane!

✿✿✿✿✿

I want to be very clear that my seven-step strategy is not intended to lock me into my plans, not allowing for spur-of-the-moment creativity flexibility, or the need to adjust for my students. It is the very opposite. Having the framework in place gives me the freedom to move things around, be creative and go with the flow. If I were planning each day or week at a time, I would have to actually work harder in the long run, experiencing frustration and anxiety along the way. With the strategies I have shared in this book, I know that I will be where I should be in order to teach the essential outcomes of curriculum in a timeframe that is best for the students – in other words, experience success in teaching with my sanity intact!

Chapter 9
And the beat goes on....

As I prepared for the start of another school year and the dreaded workshop-day discussion of how far we each got last year, I had thought that I would likely come across situations in which this book would be helpful. I have been surprised, however, at how often each chapter of this book could have been used to help a variety of teachers and administrators during this first workshop week of school! I have found myself saying to the colleagues in my department, "That's in my book!" several times a day in almost every conversation and context!

Most of the members of my department have adopted most of these steps most of the time as *the* way to implement curriculum. It is a blessing to work in a department where the ideologies mesh and where one is not afraid to work together, ask for help or give suggestions. I am delighted that I have had a hand in the development of this department and the way we have worked throughout these last few years as a team.

As I prepare to leave the classroom for good, it is personally rewarding to know that these steps have permeated our department and will likely go on as the expected way to implement curriculum in a sane manner --- my legacy of 34 years.

It also gratifying to watch these strategies spreading throughout the school district. Some teachers from my department over the years have moved to one or the other of our high schools, bringing the ideas from our school to theirs. Slowly but surely, these strategies for success are seeping into the language departments at the other schools.   It is gratifying to know that my persistence in seeking and developing these strategies in an effort to improve student learning while keeping my sanity is beginning to infiltrate the very schools that spurned my ideas 30 years ago. Ironically, the way that "Mary does it" is becoming a good thing!

In my experience, most teachers could use and would welcome suggestions that believe would help to make their teaching life more sane while delivering better instruction for more successful results. I'm convinced that the strategies based on backward planning that I have described in this book are as pertinent for curriculum implementation now as when I started to explore, adopt and adapt them 30 years ago . I know that they have worked for me and for others who have worked with me. I am sure that if all of us could look at what we are doing in a holistic manner, identify the essential outcomes, pencil in appropriate assessments, skim the cream from the textbook and then put the book back in the closet, plan out a full week at a time as best we can so we really know that we are going where we intend to go, and make notes to remind us of what to do better next year, all of us can experience success with sanity in the classroom!

❊❊❊❊❊

And now (deep breath), to walk into this year's district-wide World Language Department workshop....

....So, how far did you get last year?.....

❊❊❊❊❊

Oh, and that third piece of advice I always give my student teachers?

Anyone can live through a Friday!

References

Bushweller, Kevin. (1997) "Teaching to the Test," *The American School Board Journal*, September issue, National School Boards Association.

Condon, M. and Schreiner, S. (1996) *Using Culture as the Core through Multiple Intelligences with Authentic Assessment.* Minneapolis, MN: Milagro Publications.

Hiebert, E.H., Valencia, S.W. and Afflerbach, P. (1994) "Definitions and perspectives," Valencia, S.W., Hiebert, E.H. and Afflerbach, P. (eds) *Authentic Reading Assessment. Practices and Possibilities.* Newark; International Reading Association.

Pearson, P. D., and S. W. Valencia. (1987). "Assessment, accountability, and professional prerogative." In J. E. Readance and S. Baldwin, eds., *Research in literacy: Merging perspectives.* Rochester, NY: National Reading Conference.

Pinto, Laura Elizabeth; McDonough, Graham P; Boyd, Dwight (2011). "High School Philosophy Teachers' Use of Textbooks: Critical Thinking or

Teaching to the Text?" *Journal of Curriculum and Instruction*, November 2011, Vol. 5, No. 2, Pp. 45-78 ISSN: 1937-3929

Simulation Learning Systems. (2001-2011) P.O. Box 910, Del Mar, CA, 92014   www.stsintl.com - www.SimulationTrainingSystems.com

Warlick, David (posted 11/29/11) "The Page is Dead! Long Live Curriculum." *2¢ Worth Teaching & Learning in the new information landscape...* http://davidwarlick.com/2cents/?p=3290#comment-503503

Wiggins, G. (1989) A true test: Toward more authentic and equitable assessment. *Phi Delta Kappan* 79, no. 7: 703–713.

Wiggins, G. P. (1993) *Assessing student performance*. San Francisco, CA: Jossey-Bass Publishers.

Wiggins,G., McTighe, J. (2001). *Understanding by Design..* PrenticeHall.

ABOUT THE AUTHOR

Mary E Condon is a National Board Certified Teacher in World Languages Other than English in the United States of America. She holds a Master's degree in Education, and Bachelor degrees in Secondary Education, Spanish Education and Elementary Education. She was instrumental in the authorization and implementation of the IB MYP and DP programmes in her Global Studies magnet school. She wrote the four-year MYP and the two-year DP Spanish B courses, developed the framework for the DP Spanish *Ab Initio* courses and has served as an Areas of Interaction specialist in her school. She is an authorized trainer, visitor and consultant for the International Baccalaureate Organization and Assistant Examiner for Spanish B.

Throughout the past 34 years as a high-school teacher in the fifth-largest school district in Minnesota, she has seen many theories come and go, and has been an integral part of the planning and/or rewriting of all Spanish courses in the district. She has mentored many new, beginning and student teachers in basic classroom survival and curriculum design and implementation. Her mission through the years has been to encourage planning for successful results in a way that maintains her sanity. Her time in the classroom is winding down, but her passion for successful teaching with sanity only grows stronger every day.